A Cynic Looks at Life

Rhonda Mohammed

Copyright © 2023 by Rhonda Mohammed.

All rights reserved.

No portion of this book may be reproduced in any form without written permission from the publisher or author, except as permitted by U.S. copyright law.

Contents

1. Civilization — 1
2. The Gift O' Gab — 9
3. Natura Benigna — 11
4. The Death Penalty — 15
5. Immortality — 23
6. Emancipated Woman — 27
7. A Mad World — 31
8. Epigrams of a Cynic — 33
About the Author — 47

I

Civilization

The question "Does civilization civilize?" is a fine example of petitio principii, and decides itself in the affirmative; for civilization must needs do that from the doing of which it has its name. But it is not necessary to suppose that he who propounds is either unconscious of his lapse in logic or desirous of digging a pitfall for the feet of those who discuss; I take it he simply wishes to put the matter in an impressive way, and relies upon a certain degree of intelligence in the interpretation.

Concerning uncivilized peoples we know but little except what we are told by travelers—who, speaking generally, can know very little but the fact of uncivilization, as shown in externals and irrelevances, and are moreover, greatly given to lying. From the savages we hear very little. Judging them in all things by our own standards in default of a knowledge of theirs, we necessarily condemn, disparage and belittle. One thing that civilization certainly has not done is to make us intelligent enough to understand that the contrary of a virtue is not necessarily a vice. Because, as a rule, we have but one wife and several mistresses each it is not certain that polygamy is everywhere—nor, for that matter, anywhere—either wrong or inexpedient. Because the brutality of the civilized slave owners and dealers created a conquering sentiment against slavery it is not intelligent to assume that slavery is a maleficent thing amongst Oriental peoples (for example) where the slave is not oppressed. Some of these same Orientals whom we are pleased to term half-civilized have no regard for truth. "Takest thou me for a Christian dog," said one of them, "that I should be the slave of my word?" So far as I can perceive, the "Christian dog" is no more the slave of his word than the True Believer, and I think the savage—allowing for the fact that his inveracity has dominion over fewer things—as great a liar as either of them. For my part, I do not know what, in all circumstances, is right or wrong; but I know that, if right, it is at least stupid, to judge an uncivilized people by the standards of morality and intelligence set up by civilized ones. Life in civilized countries is so complex that men there have more ways to be good than savages have, and more to be bad; more to be happy, and more to be miserable. And in each way to be good or bad, their generally superior knowledge—their knowledge of more things—enables them to commit greater excesses than the savage can. The civilized philanthropist wreaks upon his fellows a ranker philanthropy, the civilized rascal a sturdier rascality. And—splendid triumph of enlightenment!—the two characters are, in civilization, frequently combined in one person.

I know of no savage custom or habit of thought which has not its mate in civilized countries. For every mischievous or absurd practice of the natural man I can name you one of ours that is essentially the same. And nearly every custom of our barbarian ancestors in historic times persists in some form today. We make ourselves look formidable in battle—for that matter, we fight. Our women paint their faces. We feel it obligatory to dress more or less alike, inventing the most ingenious reasons for doing so and actually despising and persecuting those who do not care to conform. Almost within the memory of living persons bearded men were stoned in the streets; and a clergyman in New York who wore his beard as Christ wore his, was put into jail and variously persecuted till he died.

Civilization does not, I think, make the race any better. It makes men know more: and if knowledge makes them happy it is useful and desirable. The one purpose of every sane human being is to be happy. No one can have any other motive than that. There is no such thing as unselfishness. We perform the most "generous" and "self-sacrificing" acts because we should be unhappy if we did not. We move on lines of least reluctance. Whatever tends to increase the beggarly sum of human happiness is worth having; nothing else has any value.

The cant of civilization fatigues. Civilization, is a fine and beautiful structure. It is as picturesque as a Gothic cathedral, but it is built upon the bones and cemented with the blood of those whose part in all its pomp is that and nothing more. It cannot be reared in the ungenerous tropics, for there the people will not contribute their blood and bones. The proposition that the average American workingman or European peasant is "better off" than the South Sea islander, lolling under a palm and drunk with over-eating, will not bear a moment's examination. It is we scholars and gentlemen that are better off.

It is admitted that the South Sea islander in a state of nature is overmuch addicted to the practice of eating human flesh; but concerning that I submit: first, that he likes it; second, that those who supply it are mostly dead. It is upon his enemies that he feeds, and these he would kill anyhow, as we do ours. In civilized, enlightened and Christian countries, where cannibalism has not yet established itself, wars are as frequent and destructive as among the maneaters. The untitled savage knows at least why he goes killing, whereas our private soldier is commonly in black ignorance of the apparent cause of quarrel—of the actual cause, always. Their shares in the fruits of victory are about equal, for the chief takes all the dead, the general all the glory.

Transplanted institutions grow slowly; civilization can not be put into a ship and carried across an ocean. The history of this country is a sequence of illustrations of these truths. It was settled by civilized men and women from civilized countries, yet after two and a half centuries, with unbroken communication with the mother systems, it is still imperfectly civilized. In learning and letters, in art and the science of government, America is but a faint and stammering echo of Europe.

For nearly all that is good in our American civilization we are indebted to the Old World; the errors and mischiefs are of our own creation. We have originated little, because there is little to originate, but we have unconsciously reproduced many of the discredited systems of former ages and other countries—receiving them at second hand, but making them ours by the sheer strength and immobility of the national belief in their novelty. Novelty! Why, it is not possible to make an experiment in government, in art, in literature, in sociology, or in morals, that has not been made over, and over, and over again.

The glories of England are our glories. She can achieve nothing that our fathers did not help to make possible to her. The learning, the power, the refinement of a great nation, are not the growth of a century, but of many centuries; each generation builds upon the work of the preceding. For untold ages our ancestors wrought to rear that "reverend pile," the civilization of England. And shall we now try to belittle the mighty structure because other though kindred hands are laying the top courses while we have elected to found a new tower in another land? The American eulogist of civilization who is not proud of his heritage in England's glory is unworthy to enjoy his lesser heritage in the lesser glory of his own country.

The English, are undoubtedly our intellectual superiors; and as the virtues are solely the product of intelligence and cultivation—a rogue being only a dunce considered from another point of view—they are our moral superiors likewise. Why should they not be? Theirs is a land, not of ugly schoolhouses grudgingly erected, containing schools supported by such niggardly tax levies as a sparse and hard-handed population will consent to pay, but of ancient institutions splendidly endowed by the state and by centuries of private benefaction. As a means of dispensing formulated ignorance our boasted public school system is not without merit; it spreads out education sufficiently thin to give everyone enough to make him a more competent fool than he would have been without it; but to compare it with that which is not the creature of legislation acting with malice aforethought, but the unnoted out-growth of ages, is to be ridiculous. It is like comparing the laid-out town of a western prairie, its right-angled streets, prim cottages, and wooden a-b-c shops, with the grand old town of Oxford, topped with the clustered domes and towers of its twenty-odd great colleges, the very names of many of whose founders have perished from human record, as have the chronicles of the times in which they lived.

It is not only that we have had to "subdue the wilderness"; our educational conditions are adverse otherwise. Our political system is unfavorable. Our fortunes, accumulated in one generation, are dispersed in the next. If it takes three generations to make a gentleman one will not make a thinker. Instruction is acquired, but capacity for instruction is transmitted. The brain that is to contain a trained intellect is not the result of a haphazard marriage between a clown and a wench, nor does it get its tractable tissues from a hard-headed farmer and a soft-headed milliner. If you confess the importance of race and pedigree in a horse and a dog how dare you deny it in a man?

I do not hold that the political and social system that creates an aristocracy of leisure is the best possible kind of human organization; I perceive its disadvantages clearly enough. But I do hold that a system under which most important public trusts, political and professional, civil and military ecclesiastical and secular, are held by educated men—that is, men of trained faculties and disciplined judgment—is not an altogether faulty system.

It is a universal human weakness to disparage the knowledge that we do not ourselves possess, but it is only my own beloved country that can justly boast herself the last refuge and asylum of the impotents and incapables who deny the advantage of all knowledge whatsoever. It was an American senator who declared that he had devoted a couple of weeks to the study of finance, and found the accepted authorities all wrong. It was another American senator who, confronted with certain hostile facts in the history of another country, proposed "to brush away all facts, and argue the question on consideration of plain common sense."

Republican institutions have this disadvantage: by incessant changes in the *personnel* of government—to say nothing of the manner of men that ignorant constituencies elect; and all constituencies are ignorant—we attain to no fixed principles and standards. There is no such thing here as a science of politics, because it is not to any one's interest to make politics the study of his life. Nothing is settled; no truth finds general acceptance. What we do one year we undo the next, and do over again the year following. Our energy is wasted in, and our prosperity suffers from, experiments endlessly repeated.

Every patriot believes his country better than any other country. Now, they cannot all be the best; indeed, only one can be the best, and it follows that the patriots of all the others have suffered themselves to be misled by a mere sentiment into blind unreason. In its active manifestation—it is fond of killing—patriotism would be well if it were simply defensive; but it is also aggressive, and the same feeling that prompts us to strike for our altars and our fires impels us over the border to quench the fires and overturn the altars of our neighbors. It is all very pretty and spirited, what the poets tell us about Thermopylæ, but there was as much patriotism at one end of that pass as there was at the other.

Patriotism deliberately and with fully aforethought subordinates the interests of a whole to the interests of a part. Worse still, the fraction so favored is determined by an accident of birth or residence. The Western hoodlum who cuts the tail from a Chinaman's nowl, and would cut the nowl from the body, if he dared, is simply a patriot with a logical mind, having the courage of his opinions. Patriotism is fierce as a fever, pitiless as the grave and blind as a stone.

There are two ways of clarifying liquids—ebullition and precipitation; one forces the impurities to the surface as scum, the other sends them to the bottom as dregs. The former is the more offensive, and that seems to be our way; but neither is useful if the impurities are merely separated but not removed. We are told with tiresome iteration that our social and political systems are clarifying; but when is the skimmer to appear? If the purpose of free institutions is good government where is the good government?—when may it be expected to begin?—how is it to come about? Systems of government have no sanctity; they are practical means to a simple end—the public welfare; worthy of no respect if they fail of its accomplishment. The tree is known by its fruit. Ours is bearing crab-apples. If the body politic is constitutionally diseased, as I verily believe; if the disorder inheres in the system; there is no remedy. The fever must burn itself out, and then Nature will do the rest. One does not prescribe what time alone can administer. We have put our criminals and dunces into power; do we suppose they will efface themselves? Will they restore to *us* the power of governing _them_? They must have their way and go their length. The natural and immemorial sequence is: tyranny, insurrection, combat. In combat everything that wears a sword has a chance—even the right. History does not forbid us to hope. But it forbids us to rely upon numbers; they will be against us. If history teaches anything worth learning it teaches that the majority of mankind is neither good nor wise. When government is founded upon the public conscience and the public intelligence the stability of states is a dream.

In that moment of time that is covered by historical records we have abundant evidence that each generation has believed itself wiser and better than any of its predecessors; that each people has believed itself to have the secret of national perpetuity. In support of this universal delusion there is nothing to be said; the desolate places of the earth cry out against it. Vestiges of obliterated civilizations cover the earth; no savage but has camped upon the sites of proud and populous cities; no desert but has heard the statesman's boast of national stability. Our nation, our laws, our history—all shall go down to everlasting oblivion with the others, and by the same road. But I submit that we are traveling it with needless haste.

It can be spared—this Jonah's gourd civilization of ours. We have hardly the rudiments of a true one; compared with the splendors of which we catch dim glimpses in the fading past, ours are as an illumination of tallow candles. We know no more than the ancients; we only know other things, but nothing in which is an assurance of perpetuity, and little that is truly wisdom. Our vaunted *elixir vitae* is the art of printing. What good will that do when posterity, struck by the inevitable intellectual blight, shall have ceased to read what is printed? Our libraries will become its stables, our books its fuel.

Ours is a civilization that might be heard from afar in space as a scolding and a riot; a civilization in which the race has so differentiated as to have no longer a community of interest and feeling; which shows as a ripe result of the principles underlying it a reasonless and rascally feud between rich and poor; in which one is offered a choice (if one have the means to take it) between American plutocracy and European militocracy, with an imminent chance of renouncing either for a stultocratic republic with a headsman in the presidential chair and every laundress in exile.

I have not a "solution" to the "labor problem." I have only a story. Many and many years ago lived a man who was so good and wise that none in all the world was so good and wise as he. He was one of those few whose goodness and wisdom are such that after some time has passed their foolish fellowmen begin to think them gods and treasure their words as divine law; and by millions they are worshiped through centuries of time. Amongst the utterances of this man was one command—not a new nor perfect one—which has seemed to his adorers so preeminently wise that they have given it a name by which it is known over half the world. One of the sovereign virtues of this famous law is its simplicity, which is such that all hearing must understand; and obedience is so easy that any nation refusing is unfit to exist except in the turbulence and adversity that will surely come to it. When a people would avert want and strife, or, having them, would restore plenty and peace, this noble commandment offers the only means—all other plans for safety or relief are as vain as dreams, as empty as the crooning of hags. And behold, here is it: "All things whatsoever ye would that men should do to you, do ye even so to them."

What! you unappeasable rich, coining the sweat and blood of your workmen into drachmas, understanding the law of supply and demand as mandatory and justifying your cruel greed by the senseless dictum that "business is business"; you lazy workmen, railing at the capitalist by whose desertion, when you have frightened away his capital, you starve—rioting and shedding blood and torturing and poisoning by way of answer to exaction and by way of exaction; you foul anarchists, applauding with untidy palms when one of your coward kind hurls a bomb amongst powerless and helpless women and children; you imbecile politicians with a plague of remedial legislation for the irremediable; you writers and thinkers unread in history, with as many "solutions to the labor problem" as there are among you those who can not coherently define it—do you really think yourselves wiser than Jesus of Nazareth? Do you seriously suppose yourselves competent to amend his plan for dealing with evils besetting nations and souls? Have you the effrontery to believe that those who spurn his Golden Rule you can bind to obedience of an act entitled an act to amend an act? Bah! you fatigue the spirit. Go get ye to your scoundrel lockouts, your villain strikes, your blacklisting, your boycotting, your speeching, marching and maundering; but if ye do not to others as ye would that they do to you it shall occur, and that right soon, that ye be drowned in your own blood and your pick-pocket civilization quenched as a star that falls into the sea.

2

The Gift O' Gab

A book entitled *Forensic Eloquence*, by Mr. John Goss, appears to have for purpose to teach the young idea how to spout, and that purpose, I dare say, it will accomplish if something is not done to prevent. I know nothing of the matter myself, a strong distaste for forensic eloquence, or eloquence of any kind implying a man mounted on his legs and doing all the talking, having averted me from its study. The training of the youth of this country to utterance of themselves after that fashion I should regard as a disaster of magnitude. So far as I know it, forensic eloquence is the art of saying things in such a way as to make them pass for more than they are worth. Employed in matters of importance (and for other employment it were hardly worth acquiring) it is mischievous because dishonest and misleading. In the public service Truth toils best when not clad in cloth-of-gold and bedaubed with fine lace. If eloquence does not beget action it is valueless; but action which results from the passions, sentiments and emotions is less likely to be wise than that which comes of a persuaded judgment. For that reason I cannot help thinking that the influence of Bismarck in German politics was more wholesome than is that of Mr. John Temple Graves.

For eloquence _per se_—considered merely as an art of pleasing—I entertain something of the respect evoked by success; for it always pleases at least the speaker. It is to speech what an ornate style is to writing—good and pleasant enough in its time and place and, like pie-crust and the evening girl, destitute of any basis in common sense. Forensic eloquence, on the contrary, has an all too sufficient foundation in reason and the order of things: it promotes the ambition of tricksters and advances the fortunes of rogues. For I take it that the Ciceros, the Mirabeaus, the Burkes, the O'Connells, the Patrick Henrys and the rest of them—pets of the text-bookers and scourges of youth—belong in either the one category or the other, or in both. Anyhow I find it impossible to think of them as highminded men and right-forth statesmen—with their actors' tricks, their devices of the countenance, inventions of gesture and other cunning expedients having nothing to do with the matter in hand. Extinction of the orator I hold to be the most beneficent possibility of evolution. If Mr. Goss has done anything to retard that blessed time when the Bourke Cockrans shall cease from troubling and the weary be at rest he is an enemy of his race.

"What!" exclaims the thoughtless reader—I have but one—"are not the great forensic speeches by the world's famous orators good reading? Considering them merely as literature do you not derive a high and refining pleasure from them?" I do not: I find them turgid and tumid no end. They are bad reading, though they may have been good hearing. In order to enjoy them one must have in memory what, indeed, one is seldom permitted to forget: that they were addressed to the ear; and in imagination one must hold some shadowy simulacrum of the orator himself, uttering his work. These conditions being fulfilled there remains for application to the matter of the discourse too little attention to get much good of it, and the total effect is confusion. Literature by which the reader is compelled to bear in mind the producer and the circumstances under which it was produced can be spared.

3

Natura Benigna

It is not always on remote islands peopled with pagans that great disasters occur, as memory witnesseth. Nor are the forces of nature inadequate to production of a fiercer throe than any that we have known. The situation is this: we are tied by the feet to a fragile shell imperfectly confining a force powerful enough under favoring conditions, to burst it asunder and set the fragments wallowing and grinding together in liquid flame, in the blind fury of a readjustment. Nay, it needs no such stupendous cataclysm to depeople this uneasy orb. Let but a square mile be blown out of the bottom of the sea, or a great rift open there. Is it to be supposed that we would be unaffected in the altered conditions generated by a contest between the ocean and the earth's molten core? These fatalities are not only possible but in the highest degree probable. It is probable, indeed, that they have occurred over and over again, effacing all the more highly organized forms of life, and compelling the slow march of evolution to begin anew. Slow? On the stage of Eternity the passing of races—the entrances and exits of Life—are incidents in a brisk and lively drama, following one another with confusing rapidity.

Mankind has not found it practicable to abandon and avoid those places where the forces of nature have been most malign. The track of the Western tornado is speedily repeopled. San Francisco is still populous, despite its earthquake, Galveston despite its storm, and even the courts of Lisbon are not kept by the lion and the lizard. In the Peruvian village straight downward into whose streets the crew of a United States warship once looked from the crest of a wave that stranded her a half mile inland are heard the tinkle of the guitar and the voices of children at play. There are people living at Herculaneum and Pompeii. On the slopes about Catania the goatherd endures with what courage he may the trembling of the ground beneath his feet as old Enceladus again turns over on his other side. As the Hoang-Ho goes back inside its banks after fertilizing its contiguity with hydrate of China-man the living agriculturist follows the receding wave, sets up his habitation beneath the broken embankment, and again the Valley of the Gone Away blossoms as the rose, its people diving with Death.

This matter can not be amended: the race exposes itself to peril because it can do no otherwise. In all the world there is no city of refuge—no temple in which to take sanctuary, clinging to the horns of the altar—no "place apart" where, like hunted deer, we can hope to elude the baying pack of Nature's malevolences. The dead-line is drawn at the gate of life: Man crosses it at birth. His advent is a challenge to the entire pack—earthquake, storm, fire, flood, drought, heat, cold, wild beasts, venomous reptiles, noxious insects, bacilli, spectacular plague and velvet-footed household disease—all are fierce and tireless in pursuit. Dodge, turn and double how he can, there's no eluding them; soon or late some of them have him by the throat and his spirit returns to the God who gave it—and gave them.

We are told that this earth was made for our inhabiting. Our dearly beloved brethren in the faith, our spiritual guides, philosophers and friends of the pulpit, never tire of pointing out the goodness of God in giving us so excellent a place to live in and commending the admirable adaptation of all things to our needs.

What a fine world it is, to be sure—a darling little world, "so suited to the needs of man." A globe of liquid fire, straining within a shell relatively no thicker than that of an egg—a shell constantly cracking and in momentary danger of going all to pieces! Three-fourths of this delectable field of human activity are covered with an element in which we can not breathe, and which swallows us by myriads:

With moldering bones the deep is white From the frozen zones to the tropic bright.

Of the other one-fourth more than one-half is uninhabitable by reason of climate. On the remaining one-eighth we pass a comfortless and precarious existence in disputed occupancy with countless ministers of death and pain—pass it in fighting for it, tooth and nail, a hopeless battle in which we are foredoomed to defeat. Everywhere death, terror, lamentation and the laughter that is more terrible than tears—the fury and despair of a race hanging on to life by the tips of its fingers. And the prize for which we strive, "to have and to hold"—what is it? A thing that is neither enjoyed while had, or missed when lost.

So worthless it is, so unsatisfying, so inadequate to purpose, so false to hope and at its best so brief, that for consolation and compensation we set up fantastic faiths of an aftertime in a better world from which no confirming whisper has ever reached us across the void. Heaven is a prophecy uttered by the lips of despair, but Hell is an inference from analogy.

4

The Death Penalty

"Down with the gallows!" is a cry not unfamiliar in America. There is always a movement afoot to make odious the just principle; of "a life for a life"—to represent it as "a relic of barbarism," "a usurpation of the divine authority," and the rest of it. The law making murder punishable by death is as purely a measure of self-defense as is the display of a pistol to one diligently endeavoring to kill without provocation. It is in precisely the same sense an admonition, a warning to abstain from crime. Society says by that law: "If you kill one of us you die," just as by display of the pistol the individual whose life is attacked says: "Desist or be shot." To be effective the warning in either case must be more than an idle threat. Even the most unearthly reasoner among the anti-hanging unfortunates would hardly expect to frighten away an assassin who knew the pistol to be unloaded. Of course these queer illogicians can not be made to understand that their position commits them to absolute non-resistance to any kind of aggression; and that is fortunate for the rest of us, for if as Christians they frankly and consistently took that ground we should be under the miserable necessity of respecting them.

We have good reason to hold that the horrible prevalence of murder in this country is due to the fact that we do not execute our laws—that the death penalty is threatened but not inflicted—that the pistol is not loaded. In civilized countries where there is enough respect for the laws to administer them, there is enough to obey them. While man still has as much of the ancestral brute as his skin can hold without cracking we shall have thieves and demagogues and anarchists and assassins and persons with a private system of lexicography who define murder as disease and hanging as murder, but in all this welter of crime and stupidity are areas where human life is comparatively secure against the human hand. It is at least a significant coincidence that in these the death penalty for murder is fairly well enforced by judges who do not derive any part of their authority from those for whose restraint and punishment they hold it. Against the life of one guiltless person the lives of ten thousand murderers count for nothing; their hanging is a public good, without reference to the crimes that disclose their deserts. If we could discover them by other signs than their bloody deeds they should be hanged anyhow. Unfortunately we must have a death as evidence. The scientist who will tell us how to recognize the potential assassin, and persuade us to kill him, will be the greatest benefactor of his century.

What would these enemies of the gibbet have—these lineal descendants of the drunken mobs that hooted the hangman at Tyburn Tree; this progeny of criminals, which has so defiled with the mud of its animosity the noble office of public, executioner that even "in this enlightened age" he shirks his high duty, entrusting it to a hidden or unnamed subordinate? If murder is unjust of what importance is it whether its punishment by death be just or not?—nobody needs to incur it. Men are not drafted for the death penalty; they volunteer. "Then it is not deterrent," mutters the gentleman whose rude forefather hooted the hangman. Well, as to that, the law which is to accomplish more than a part of its purpose must be awaited with great patience. Every murder proves that hanging is not altogether deterrent; every hanging, that it is somewhat deterrent—it deters the person hanged. A man's first murder is his crime, his second is ours.

The socialists, it seems, believe with Alphonse Karr, in the expediency of abolishing the death penalty; but apparently they do not hold, with him, that the assassins should begin. They want the state to begin, believing that the magnanimous example will effect a change of heart in those about to murder. This, I take it, is the meaning of their assertion that death penalties have not the deterring influence that imprisonment for life carries. In this they obviously err: death deters at least the person who suffers it—he commits no more murder; whereas the assassin who is imprisoned for life and immune from further punishment may with impunity kill his keeper or whomsoever he may be able to get at. Even as matters now are, incessant vigilance is required to prevent convicts in prison from murdering their attendants and one another. How would it be if the "life-termer" were assured against any additional inconvenience for braining a guard occasionally, or strangling a chaplain now and then? A penitentiary may be described as a place of punishment and reward; and under the system proposed, the difference in desirableness between a sentence and an appointment would be virtually effaced. To overcome this objection a life sentence would have to mean solitary confinement, and that means insanity. Is that what these gentlemen propose to substitute for death?

The death penalty, say these amiables and futilitarians, creates blood-thirstiness in the unthinking masses and defeats its own ends—is itself a cause of murder, not a check. These gentlemen are themselves of "the unthinking masses"—they do not know how to think. Let them try to trace and lucidly expound the chain of motives lying between the knowledge that a murderer has been hanged and the wish to commit a murder. How, precisely, does the one beget the other? By what unearthly process of reasoning does a man turning away from the gallows persuade himself that it is expedient to incur the danger of hanging? Let us have pointed out to us the several steps in that remarkable mental progress. Obviously, the thing is absurd; one might as reasonably say that contemplation of a pitted face will make a man wish to go and catch smallpox, or the spectacle of an amputated limb on the scrap-heap of a hospital tempt him to cut off his arm or renounce his leg.

"An eye for an eye and a tooth for a tooth," say the opponents of the death penalty, "is not justice; it is revenge and unworthy of a Christian civilization." It is exact justice: nobody can think of anything more accurately just than such punishments would be, whatever the motive in awarding them. Unfortunately such a system is not practicable, but he who denies its justice must deny also the justice of a bushel of corn for a bushel of corn, a dollar for a dollar, service for service. We can not undertake by such clumsy means as laws and courts to do to the criminal exactly "what he has done to his victim, but to demand a life for a life is simple, practicable, expedient and (therefore) right.

"Taking the life of a murderer does not restore the life he took, therefore it is a most illogical punishment. Two wrongs do not make a right."

Here's richness! Hanging an assassin is illogical because it does not restore the life of his victim; incarceration is logical; therefore, incarceration does—_quod, erat demonstrandum._

Two wrongs certainly do not make a right, but the veritable thing in dispute is whether taking the life of a life-taker is a wrong. So naked and unashamed an example of *petitio principii* would disgrace a debater in a pinafore. And these wonder-mongers have the effrontery to babble of "logic"! Why, if one of them were to meet a syllogism in a lonely road he would run away in a hundred and fifty directions as hard as ever he could hoof it. One is almost ashamed to dispute with such intellectual cloutlings.

Whatever an individual may rightly do to protect himself society may rightly do to protect him, for he is a part of itself. If he may rightly take life in defending himself society may rightly take life in defending him. If society may rightly take life in defending him it may rightly threaten to take it. Having rightly and mercifully threatened to take it, it not only rightly may take it, but expediently must.

The law of a life for a life does not altogether prevent murder. No law can altogether prevent any form of crime, nor is it desirable that it should. Doubtless God could so have created us that our sense of right and justice could have existed without contemplation of injustice and wrong; as doubtless he could so have created us that we could have felt compassion without a knowledge of suffering; but he did not. Constituted as we are, we can know good only by contrast with evil. Our sense of sin is what our virtues feed upon; in the thin air of universal morality the altar-fires of honor and the beacons of conscience could not be kept alight. A community without crime would be a community without warm and elevated sentiments—without the sense of justice, without generosity, without courage, without mercy, without magnanimity—a community of small, smug souls, uninteresting to God and uncoveted by the Devil. We can have, and do have, too much crime, no doubt; what the wholesome proportion is none can tell. Just now we are running a good deal to murder, but he who can gravely attribute that phenomenon, or any part of it, to infliction of the death penalty, instead of to virtual immunity from any penalty at all, is justly entitled to the innocent satisfaction that comes of being a simpleton.

The New Woman is against the death penalty, naturally, for she is hot and hardy in the conviction that whatever is is wrong. She has visited this world in order to straighten things about a bit, and is in distress lest the number of things be insufficient to her need.

The matter is important variously; not least so in its relation to the new heaven and the new earth that are to be the outcome of woman suffrage. There can be no doubt that the vast majority of women have sentimental objections to the death penalty that quite outweigh such practical considerations in its favor as they can be persuaded to comprehend. Aided by the minority of men afflicted by the same mental malady, they will indubitably effect its abolition in the first lustrum of their political "equality." The New Woman will scarcely feel the seat of power warm beneath her before giving to the assassin's "unhand me, villain!" the authority of law. So we shall make again the old experiment, discredited by a thousand failures, of preventing crime by tenderness to caught criminals. And the criminal uncaught will treat us to a quantity and quality of crime notably augmented by the Christian spirit of the new régime.

As to painless execution, the simple and practical way to make them both just and expedient is the adoption by murderers of a system of painless assassinations. Until this is done there seems to be no call to renounce the wholesome discomfort of the style of executions endeared to us by memories and associations of the tenderest character. There is, I fancy, a shaping notion in the observant mind that the penologists and their allies have gone about as far as they can safely be permitted to go in the direction of a softer suasion of the criminal nature toward good behavior. The modern prison has become a rather more comfortable habitation than the dangerous classes are accustomed to at home. Modern prison life has in their eyes something of the charm and glamor of an ideal existence, like that in the Happy Valley from which Rasselas had the folly to escape. Whatever advantages to the public may be secured by abating the rigors of imprisonment and inconveniences incident to execution, there is this objection: it makes them less deterrent. Let the penologers and philanthropers have their way and even hanging might be made so pleasant and withal so interesting a social distinction that it would deter nobody but the person hanged. Adopt the euthanasian method of electricity, asphyxia by smothering in rose-leaves, or slow poisoning with rich food, and the death penalty may come to be regarded as the object of a noble ambition to the *bon vivant,* and the rising young suicide may go and kill somebody else instead of himself, in order to receive from the public executioner a happier dispatch than his own 'prentice hand can assure him.

But the advocates of agreeable pains and penalties tell us that in the darker ages, when cruel and degrading punishment was the rule, and was freely inflicted for every light infraction of the law, crime was more common than it is now; and in this they appear to be right. But one and all, they overlook a fact equally obvious and vastly significant, that the intellectual, moral and social condition of the masses was very low. Crime was more common because ignorance was more common, poverty was more common, sins of authority, and therefore hatred of authority, were more common. The world of even a century ago was a different world from the world of today, and a vastly more uncomfortable one. The popular adage to the contrary notwithstanding, human nature was not by a long cut the same then that it is now. In the very ancient time of that early English king, George III, when women were burned at the stake in public for various offenses and men were hanged for "coining" and children for theft, and in the still remoter period (*circa* 1530), when prisoners were boiled in several waters, divers sorts of criminals were disemboweled and some are thought to have undergone the *peine forte et dure* of cold-pressing (an infliction which the pen of Hugo has since made popular—in literature)—in these wicked old days crime flourished, not because of the law's severity, but in spite of it. It is possible that our law-making ancestors understood the situation as it then was a trifle better than we can understand it on the hither side of this gulf of years, and that they were not the reasonless barbarians that we think them to have been. And if they were, what must have been the unreason and barbarity of the criminal element with which they had to deal?

I am far from thinking that severity of punishment can have the same restraining effect as probability of some punishment being inflicted; but if mildness of penalty is to be superadded to difficulty of conviction, and both are to be mounted upon laxity in detection, the pile will be complete indeed. There is a peculiar fitness, perhaps, in the fact that all these pleas for comfortable punishment should be urged at a time when there appears to be a general disposition to inflict no punishment at all. There are, however, still a few old-fashioned persons who hold it obvious that one who is ambitious to break the laws of his country will not with so light a heart and so airy an indifference incur the peril of a harsh penalty as he will the chance of one more nearly resembling that which he would himself select.

After lying for more than a century dead I was revived, dowered with a new body, and restored to society. The first thing of interest that I observed was an enormous building, covering a square mile of ground. It was surrounded on all sides by a high, strong wall of hewn stone upon which armed sentinels paced to and fro. In one face of the wall was a single gate of massive iron, strongly guarded. While admiring the Cyclopean architecture of the "reverend pile" I was accosted by a man in uniform, evidently the warden, with a cheerful salutation.

"Colonel," I said, "pray tell me what is this building."

"This," said he, "is the new state penitentiary. It is one of twelve, all alike."

"You surprise me," I replied. "Surely the criminal element must have increased enormously."

"Yes, indeed," he assented; "under the Reform _régime_, which began in your day, crime became so powerful, bold and fierce that arrests were no longer possible and the prisons then in existence were soon overcrowded. The state was compelled to erect others of greater capacity."

"But, Colonel," I protested, "if the criminals were too bold and powerful to be taken into custody, of what use are the prisons? And how are they crowded?"

He fixed upon me a look that I could not fail to interpret as expressing a doubt of my sanity. "What!" he said, "is it possible that the modern penology is unknown to you? Do you suppose we practice the antiquated and ineffective method of shutting up the rascals? Sir, the growth of the criminal element has, as I said, compelled the erection of more and larger prisons. We have enough to hold comfortably all the honest men and women of the state. Within these protecting walls they carry on all the necessary vocations of life excepting commerce. That is necessarily in the hands of the rogues, as before."

"Venerated representative of Reform," I exclaimed, wringing his hand with effusion, "you are Knowledge, you are History, you are the Higher Education! We must talk further.

Come, let us enter this benign edifice; you shall show me your dominion and instruct me in the rules. You shall propose me as an inmate."

I walked rapidly to the gate. When challenged by the sentinel, I turned to summon my instructor. He was nowhere visible. I turned again to look at the prison. Nothing was there: desolate and forbidding, as about the broken statue of Ozymandias.

The lone and level sands stretched far away.

5

Immortality

The desire for life everlasting has commonly been affirmed to be universal—at least that is the view taken by those unacquainted with Oriental faiths and with Oriental character. Those of us whose knowledge is a trifle wider are not prepared to say that the desire is universal nor even general.

If the devout Buddhist, for example, wishes to "live always," he has not succeeded in very clearly formulating the desire. The sort of thing that he is pleased to hope for is not what we should call life, and not what many of us would care for.

When a man says that everybody has "a horror of annihilation," we may be very sure that he has not many opportunities for observation, or that he has not availed himself of all that he has. Most persons go to sleep rather gladly, yet sleep is virtual annihilation while it lasts; and if it should last forever the sleeper would be no worse off after a million years of it than after an hour of it. There are minds sufficiently logical to think of it that way, and to them annihilation is not a disagreeable thing to contemplate and expect.

In this matter of immortality, people's beliefs appear to go along with their wishes. The man who is content with annihilation thinks he will get it; those that want immortality are pretty sure they are immortal; and that is a very comfortable allotment of faiths. The few of us that are left unprovided for are those who do not bother themselves much about the matter, one way or another.

The question of human immortality is the most momentous that the mind is capable of conceiving. If it is a fact that the dead live all other facts are in comparison trivial and without interest. The prospect of obtaining certain knowledge with regard to this stupendous matter is not encouraging. In all countries but those in barbarism the powers of the profoundest and most penetrating intelligences have been ceaselessly addressed to the task of glimpsing a life beyond this life; yet today no one can truly say that he knows. It is as much a matter of faith as ever it was.

Our modern Christian nations profess a passionate hope and belief in another world, yet the most popular writer and speaker of his time, the man whose lectures drew the largest audiences, the work of whose pen brought him the highest rewards, was he who most strenuously strove to destroy the ground of that hope and unsettle the foundations of that belief.

The famous and popular Frenchman, Professor of Spectacular Astronomy, Camille Flammarion, affirms immortality because he has talked with departed souls who said that it was true. Yes, monsieur, but surely you know the rule about hearsay evidence. We Anglo-Saxons are very particular about that.

M. Flammarion says:

"I don't repudiate the presumptive arguments of schoolmen. I merely supplement them with something positive. For instance, if you assumed the existence of God this argument of the scholastics is a good one. God has implanted in all men the desire of perfect happiness. This desire cannot be satisfied in our lives here. If there were not another life wherein to satisfy it then God would be a declever. *Voila tout.*"

There is more: the desire of perfect happiness does not imply immortality, even if there is a God, for

(1) God may not have implanted it, but merely suffers it to exist, as he suffers sin to exist, the desire of wealth, the desire to live longer than we do in this world. It is not held that God implanted all the desires of the human heart. Then /why hold that he implanted that of perfect happiness?

(2) Even if he did—even, if a divinely implanted desire entail its own gratification—even if it cannot be gratified in this life—that does not imply immortality. It implies *only* another life long enough for its gratification just once. An eternity of gratification is not a logical inference from it.

(3) Perhaps God *is* "a deceiver" who knows that he is not? Assumption of the existence of a God is one thing; assumption of the existence of a God who is honorable and candid according to our conception of honor and candor is another.

(4) There may be an honorable and candid God. He may have implanted in us the desire of perfect happiness. It may be—it is—impossible to gratify that desire in this life. Still, another life is not implied, for God may not have intended us to draw the inference that he is going to gratify it. If omniscient and omnipotent, God must be held to have intended whatever occurs, but no such God is assumed in M. Flammarion's illustration, and it may be that God's knowledge and power are limited, or that one of them is limited.

M. Flammarion is a learned, if somewhat theatrical, astronomer. He has a tremendous imagination, which naturally is more at home in the marvelous and catastrophic than in the orderly regions of familiar phenomena. To him the heavens are an immense pyrotechnicon and he is the master of the show and sets off the fireworks. But he knows nothing of logic, which is the science of straight thinking, and his views of things have therefore no value; they are nebulous.

Nothing is clearer than that our pre-existence is a dream, having absolutely no basis in anything that we know or can hope to know. Of after-existence there is said to be evidence, or rather testimony, in assurances of those who are in present enjoyment of it—if it is enjoyable. Whether this testimony has actually been given—and it is the only testimony worth a moment's consideration—is a disputed point. Many persons living this life profess to have received it. But nobody professes, or ever has professed, to have received a communication of any kind from one in actual experience of the fore-life. "The souls as yet ungarmented," if such there are, are dumb to question. The Land beyond the Grave has been, if not observed, yet often and variously described: if not explored and surveyed, yet carefully charted. From among so many accounts of it that we have, he must be fastidious indeed who cannot be suited. But of the Fatherland that spreads before the cradle—the great Heretofore, wherein we all dwelt if we are to dwell in the Hereafter, we have no account. Nobody professes knowledge of that. No testimony reaches our ears of flesh concerning its topographical or other features; no one has been so enterprising as to wrest from its actual inhabitants any particulars of their character and appearance. And among educated experts and professional proponents of worlds to be there is a general denial of its existence.

I am of their way of thinking about that. The fact that we have no recollection of a former life is entirely conclusive of the matter. To have lived an unrecollected life is impossible and unthinkable, for there would be nothing to connect the new life with the old—no thread of continuity—nothing that persisted from the one life to the other. The later birth would be that of another person, an altogether different being, unrelated to the first—a new John Smith succeeding to the late Tom Jones.

Let us not be misled here by a false analogy. Today I may get a thwack o' the mazzard which will give me an intervening season of unconsciousness between yesterday and to-morrow. Thereafter I may live to a green old age with no recollection of anything that I knew, or did, or was before the accident; yet I shall be the same person, for between the old life and the new there will be a *nexus*, a thread of continuity, something spanning the gulf from the one state to the other, and the same in both—namely, my body with its habits, capacities and powers. That is I; that identifies me to others as my former self—authenticates and credentials me as the person that incurred the cranial mischance, dislodging memory.

But when death occurs *all* is dislodged if memory is; for between two merely mental or spiritual existences memory is the only *nexus* conceivable; consciousness of identity is the only identity. To live again without memory of having lived before is to live another. Re-existence without recollection is absurd. There is nothing to re-exist.

6

Emancipated Woman

What I should like to know is, how "the enlargement of woman's sphere" by her entrance into various activities of commercial, professional and industrial life benefits the sex. It may please Helen Gougar and satisfy her sense of logical accuracy to say, as she does: "We women must work in order to fill the places left vacant by liquor-drinking men." But who filled these places before? Did they remain vacant, or were there then disappointed applicants, as now? If my memory serves, there has been no time in the period that it covers when the supply of workers—abstemious male workers—was not in excess of the demand. That it has always been so is sufficiently attested by the universally inadequate wage rate.

Employers seldom fail, and never for long, to get all the workmen they need. The field into which women have put their sickles was already overcrowded with reapers. Whatever employment women have obtained has been got by displacing men—who would otherwise be supporting women.; Where is the general advantage? We may shout "high tariff," "combination of capital," "demonetization of silver," and what not, but if searching for the cause of augmented poverty and crime, "industrial discontent" and the tramp evil, instead of dogmatically expounding it, we should take some account of this enormous, sudden addition to the number of workers seeking work. If any one thinks that within the brief period of a generation the visible supply of labor can be enormously augmented without profoundly affecting the stability of things and disastrously touching the interests of wage-workers let no rude voice dispel his dream of such maleficent agencies as his slumbrous understanding may joy to affirm. And let our Widows of Ashur unlung themselves in advocacy of quack remedies for evils of which themselves are cause; it remains true that when the contention of two lions for one bone is exacerbated by the accession of a lioness the squabble is not composable by stirring up some bears in the cage adjacent.

Indubitably a woman is under no obligation to sacrifice herself to the good of her sex by foregoing needed employment in the hope that it may fall to a man gifted with dependent women. Nevertheless our congratulations are more intelligent when bestowed upon her individual head than when sifted into the hair of all Eve's daughters. This is a world of complexities, in which the lines of interest are so intertangled as frequently to transgress that of sex; and one ambitious to help but half the race may profitably know that every effort to that end provokes a counterbalancing mischief. The "enlargement of woman's opportunities" has benefited individual women. It has not benefited the sex as a whole, and has distinctly damaged the race. The mind that can not discern a score of great and irreparable general evils distinctly traceable to "emancipation of woman" is as impregnable to the light as a toad in a rock.

A marked demerit of the new order of things—the _régime_ of female commercial service—is that its main advantage accrues, not to the race, not to the sex, not to the class, not to the individual woman, but to the person of least need and worth—the male employer. (Female employers in any considerable number there will not be, but those that we have could give the male ones profitable instruction in grinding the faces of their employes.) This constant increase of the army of labor—always and everywhere too large for the work in sight—by accession of a new contingent of natural oppressibles makes the very teeth of old Munniglut thrill with a poignant delight. It brings in that situation known as two laborers seeking one job—and one of them a person whose bones he can easily grind to make his bread; and Munniglut is a miller of skill and experience, dusted all over with the evidence of his useful craft. When Heaven has assisted the Daughters of Hope to open to women a new "avenue of opportunities" the first to enter and walk therein, like God in the Garden of Eden, is the good Mr. Munniglut, contentedly smoothing the folds out of the superior slope of his paunch, exuding the peculiar aroma of his oleaginous personality and larding the new roadway with the overflow of a righteousness stimulated to action by relish of his own identity. And ever thereafter the subtle suggestion of a fat philistinism lingers along that path of progress like an assertion of a possessory right.

It is God's own crystal truth that in dealing with women unfortunate enough to be compelled to earn their own living and fortunate enough to have wrested from Fate an opportunity to do so, men of business and affairs treat them with about the same delicate consideration that they show to dogs and horses of the inferior breeds. It does not commonly occur to the wealthy "professional man," or "prominent merchant," to be ashamed to add to his yearly thousands a part of the salary justly due to his female bookkeeper or typewriter, who sits before him all day with an empty belly in order to have an habilimented back. He has a vague, hazy notion that the law of supply and demand is mandatory, and that in submitting himself to it by paying her a half of what he would have to pay a man of inferior efficiency he is supplying the world with a noble example of obedience. I must take the liberty to remind him that the law of supply and demand is not imperative; it is not a statute but a phenomenon. He may reply: "It is imperative; the penalty for disobedience is failure. If I pay more in salaries and wages than I need to, my competitor will not; and with that advantage he will drive me from the field." If his margin of profit is so small that he must eke it out by coining the sweat of his workwomen into nickels I've nothing to say to him. Let him adopt in peace the motto, "I cheat to eat." I do not know why he should eat, but Nature, who has provided sustenance for the worming sparrow, the sparrowing owl and the owling eagle, approves the needy man of prey and makes a place for him at table.

Human nature is pretty well balanced; for every lacking virtue there is a rough substitute that will serve at a pinch—as cunning is the wisdom of the unwise, and ferocity the courage of the coward. Nobody is altogether bad; the scoundrel who has grown rich by underpaying workmen in his factory will sometimes endow an asylum for indigent seamen. To oppress one's own workmen, and provide for the workmen of a neighbor—to skin those in charge of one's own interests while cottoning and oiling the residuary product of another's skinnery—that is not very good benevolence, nor very good sense, but it serves in place of both. The man who eats _pâté de fois gras_ in the sweat of his girl cashier's face, or wears purple and fine linen in order that his typewriter may have an eocene gown and a pliocene hat, seems a tolerably satisfactory specimen of the genus thief; but let us not forget that in his own home—a fairly good one—he may enjoy and merit that highest and most honorable title on the scroll of woman's favor, "a good provider." One having a claim to that glittering distinction should enjoy immunity from the coarse and troublesome question, "From whose backs and bellies do you provide?"

So much for the material results to the sex. What are the moral results? One does not like to speak of them, particularly to those who do not and can not know—to good women in whose innocent minds female immorality is inseparable from flashy gowning and the painted face; to foolish, book-taught men who honestly believe in some protective sanctity that hedges womanhood. If men of the world with years enough to have lived out of the old _régime_ into the new would testify in this matter there would ensue a great rattling of dry bones in bodices of reform-ladies. Nay, if the young man about town, knowing nothing of how things were in the "dark backward and absym of time," but something of the moral distance between even so free-running a creature as the society girl and the average working girl of the factory, the shop and the office, would speak out (under assurance of immunity from prosecution) his testimony would be a surprise to the cartilaginous virgins, blowsy matrons, acrid relicts and hairy males of Emancipation. It would pain, too, some very worthy but unobservant persons not in sympathy with "the cause."

Certain significant facts are within the purview of all but the very young and the comfortably blind. To the woman of to-day the man of to-day is imperfectly polite. In place of reverence lie gives her "deference"; to the language of compliment has succeeded the language of raillery. Men have almost forgotten how to bow. Doubtless the advanced female prefers the new manner, as may some of her less forward sisters, thinking it more sincere. It is not; our giddy grandfather talked high-flown nonsense because his heart had tangled his tongue. He treated his woman more civilly than we ours because he loved her better. He never had seen her on the "rostrum" and in the lobby, never had heard her in advocacy of herself, never had read her confessions of his sins, never had felt the stress of her competition, nor himself assisted by daily personal contact in rubbing the bloom off her. He did not know that her virtues were due to her secluded life, but thought, dear old boy, that they were a gift of God.

7

A Mad World

Let us suppose that in tracing its cycloidal curves through the unthinkable reaches of space traversed by the solar system our planet should pass through a "belt" of attenuated matter having the property of dementing us! It is a conception easily enough entertained. That space is full of malign conditions incontinuously distributed; that we are at one time traversing a zone comparatively innocuous and at another spinning through a region of infection; that away behind us in the wake of our swirling flight are fields of plague and pain still agitated by our passage through them,—all this is as good as known. It is almost as certain as it is that in our little annual circle round the sun are points at which we are stoned and brick-batted like a pig in a potato-patch—pelted with little nodules of meteoric metal flung like gravel, and bombarded with gigantic masses hurled by God knows what? What strange adventures await us in those yet untraveled regions toward which we speed?—into what malign conditions may we not at any time plunge?—to the strength and stress of what frightful environment may we not at last succumb? The subject lends itself readily enough to a jest, but I am not jesting: it is really altogether probable that our solar system, racing through space with inconceivable velocity, will one day enter a region charged with something deleterious to the human brain, minding us all mad-wise.

By the way, dear reader, did you ever happen to consider the possibility that you are a lunatic, and perhaps confined in an asylum? It seems to you that you are not—that you go with freedom where you will, and use a sweet reasonableness in all your works and ways; but to many a lunatic it seems that he is Rameses II, or the Holkar of Indore. Many a plunging maniac, ironed to the floor of a cell, believes himself the Goddess of Liberty careering gaily through the Ten Commandments in a chariot of gold. Of your own sanity and identity you have no evidence that is any better than he has of his. More accurately, I have none of mine; for anything I know, you do not exist, nor any one of all the things with which I think myself familiarly conscious. All may be fictions of my disordered imagination. I really know of but one reason for doubting that I am an inmate of an asylum for the insane—namely, the probability that there is nowhere any such thing as an asylum for the insane.

This kind of speculation has charms that get a good neck-hold upon attention. For example, if I am really a lunatic, and the persons and things that I seem to see about me have no objective existence, what an ingenious though disordered imagination I must have! What a clever *coup* it was to invent Mr. Rockefeller and clothe him with the attribute of permanence! With what amusing qualities I have endowed my laird of Skibo, philanthropist. What a masterpiece of creative humor is my Fatty Taft, statesman, taking himself seriously, even solemnly, and persuading others to do the same! And this city of Washington, with its motley population of silurians, parvenoodles and scamps pranking unashamed in the light of day, and its saving contingent of the forsaken righteous, their seed begging bread,—did Rabelais' exuberant fancy ever conceive so—but Rabelais is, perhaps, himself a conception.

Surely he is no common maniac who has wrought out of nothing the history, the philosophies, sciences, arts, laws, religions, politics and morals of this imaginary world. Nay, the world itself, tumbling uneasily through space like a beetle's ball, is no mean achievement, and I am proud of it. But the mental feat in which I take most satisfaction, and which I doubt not is most diverting to my keepers, is that of creating Mr. W.R. Hearst, pointing his eyes toward the White House and endowing him with a perilous Jacksonian ambition to defile it. The Hearst is distinctly a treasure.

On the whole, I have done, I think, tolerably well, and when I contemplate the fertility and originality of my inventions, the queer unearthliness and grotesque actions of the characters whom I have evolved, isolated and am cultivating, I cannot help thinking that if Heaven had not made me a lunatic my peculiar talent might have made me an entertaining writer.

8

Epigrams of a Cynic

If every hypocrite in the United States were to break his leg to-day the country could be successfully invaded to-morrow by the warlike hypocrites of Canada.

To Dogmatism the Spirit of Inquiry is the same as the Spirit of Evil, and to pictures of the latter it appends a tail to represent the note of interrogation.

"Immoral" is the judgment of the stalled ox on the gamboling lamb.

In forgiving an injury be somewhat ceremonious, lest your magnanimity be construed as indifference.

True, man does not know woman. But neither does woman.

Age is provident because the less future we have the more we fear it.

Reason is fallible and virtue invincible; the winds vary and the needle forsakes the pole, but stupidity never errs and never intermits. Since it has been found that the axis of the earth wabbles, stupidity is indispensable as a standard of constancy.

In order that the list of able women may be memorized for use at meetings of the oppressed sex, Heaven has considerately made it brief.

Firmness is my persistency; obstinacy is yours.

A little heap of dust, A little streak of rust, A stone without a name— Lo! hero, sword and fame.

Our vocabulary is defective; we give the same name to woman's lack of temptation and man's lack of opportunity.

"You scoundrel, you have wronged me," hissed the philosopher. "May you live forever!"

The man who thinks that a garnet can be made a ruby by setting it in brass is writing "dialect" for publication.

"Who art thou, stranger, and what dost thou seek?" "I am Generosity, and I seek a person named Gratitude." "Then thou dost not deserve to find her." "True. I will go about my business and think of her no more. But who art thou, to be so wise?" "I am Gratitude—farewell forever."

There was never a genius who was not thought a fool until he disclosed himself; whereas he is a fool then only.

The boundaries that Napoleon drew have been effaced; the kingdoms that he set up have disappeared. But all the armies and statecraft of Europe cannot unsay what you have said.

Strive not for singularity in dress; Fools have the more and men of sense the less. To look original is not worth while, But be in mind a little out of style.

A conqueror arose from the dead. "Yesterday," he said, "I ruled half the world." "Please show me the half that you ruled," said an angel, pointing out a wisp of glowing vapor floating in space. "That is the world."

"Who art thou, shivering in thy furs?" "My name is Avarice. What is thine?" "Unselfishness." "Where is thy clothing, placid one?" "Thou art wearing it."

To be comic is merely to be playful, but wit is a serious matter. To laugh at it is to confess that you do not understand.

If you would be accounted great by your contemporaries, be not too much greater than they.

To have something that he will not desire, nor know that he has—such is the hope of him who seeks the admiration of posterity. The character of his work does not matter; he is a humorist.

Women, and foxes, being weak, are distinguished by superior tact.

To fatten pigs, confine and feed them; to fatten rogues, cultivate a generous disposition.

Every heart is the lair of a ferocious animal. The greatest wrong that you can put upon a man is to provoke him to let out his beast.

When two irreconcilable propositions are presented for assent the safest way is to thank Heaven that we are not as the unreasoning brutes, and believe both.

Truth is more deceptive than falsehood, for it is more frequently presented by those from whom we do not expect it, and so has against it a numerical presumption.

A bad marriage is like an electrical thrilling machine: it makes you dance, but you can't let go.

Meeting Merit on a street-crossing, Success stood still. Merit stepped off into the mud and went around him, bowing his apologies, which Success had the grace to accept.

"I think," says the philosopher divine, "Therefore I am." Sir, here's a surer sign: We know we live, for with our every breath we feel the fear and imminence of death.

The first man you meet is a fool. If you do not think so ask him and he will prove it.

He who would rather inflict injustice than suffer it will always have his choice, for no injustice can be done to him.

There are as many conceptions of a perfect happiness hereafter as there are minds that have marred their happiness here.

We yearn to be, not what we are, but what we are not. If we were immortal we should not crave immortality.

A rabbit's foot may bring good luck to you, but it brought none to the rabbit.

Before praising the wisdom of the man who knows how to hold his tongue ascertain if he knows how to hold his pen.

The most charming view in the world is obtained by introspection.

Love is unlike chess, in that the pieces are moved secretly and the player sees most of the game. But the looker-on has one incomparable advantage: he is not the stake.

It is not for nothing that tigers choose to hide in the jungle, for commerce and trade are carried on, mostly, in the open.

We say that we love, not whom we will, but whom we must. Our judgment need not, therefore, go to confession.

Of two kinds of temporary insanity, one ends in suicide, the other in marriage.

If you give alms from compassion, why require the beneficiary to be "a deserving object?" No other adversity is so sharp as destitution of merit.

Bereavement is the name that selfishness gives to a particular privation.

O proud philanthropist, your hope is vain To get by giving what you lost by gain. With every gift you do but swell the cloud Of witnesses against you, swift and loud— Accomplices who turn and swear you split Your life: half robber and half hypocrite. You're least unsafe when most intact you hold Your curst allotment of dishonest gold.

The highest and rarest form of contentment is aproval of the success of another.

If Inclination challenge, stand and fight— From Opportunity the wise take flight.

What a woman most admires in a man is distinction among men. What a man most admires in a woman is devotion to himself.

Those who most loudly invite God's attention to themselves when in peril of death are those who should most fervently wish to escape his observation.

When you have made a catalogue of your friend's faults it is only fair to supply him with a duplicate, so that he may know yours.

How fascinating is Antiquity!—in what a golden haze the ancients lived their lives! We, too, are ancients. Of our enchanting time Posterity's great poets will sing immortal songs, and its archaeologists will reverently uncover the foundations of our palaces and temples.

Meantime we swap jack-knives.

Observe, my son, with how austere a virtue the man without a cent puts aside the temptation to manipulate the market or acquire a monopoly.

For study of the good and the bad in woman two women are a needless expense.

"There's no free will," says the philosopher; "To hang is most unjust." "There is no free will," assents the officer; "We hang because we must."

Hope is an explorer who surveys the country ahead. That is why we know so much about the Hereafter and so little about the Heretofore.

Remembering that it was a woman who lost the world, we should accept the act of cackling geese in saving Rome as partial reparation.

There are two classes of women who may do as they please; those who are rich and those who are poor. The former can count on assent, the latter on inattention.

When into the house of the heart Curiosity is admitted as the guest of Love she turns her host out of doors.

Happiness has not to all the same name: to Youth she is known as the Future; Age knows her as the Dream.

"Who art thou, there in the mire?" "Intuition. I leaped all the way from, where thou standest in fear on the brink of the bog." "A great feat, madam; accept the admiration of Reason, sometimes known as Dryfoot."

In eradicating an evil, it makes a difference whether it is uprooted or rooted up. The difference is in the reformer.

The Audible Sisterhood rightly affirms the equality of the sexes: no man is so base but some woman is base enough to love him.

Having no eyes in the back of the head, we see ourselves on the verge of the outlook. Only he who has accomplished the notable feat of turning about knows himself the central figure in the universe.

Truth is so good a thing that falsehood can not afford to be without it.

If women did the writing of the world, instead of the talking, men would be regarded as the superior sex in beauty, grace and goodness.

Love is a delightful day's journey. At the farther end kiss your companion and say farewell.

Let him who would wish to duplicate his every experience prate of the value of life.

The game of discontent has its rules, and he who disregards them cheats. It is not permitted to you to wish to add another's advantages or possessions to your own; you are permitted only to wish to be another.

The creator and arbiter of beauty is the heart; to the male rattlesnake the female rattlesnake is the loveliest thing in nature.

Thought and emotion dwell apart. When the heart goes into the head there is no dissension; only an eviction.

If you want to read a perfect book there is only one way: write it.

"Where goest thou, Ignorance?" "To fortify the mind of a maiden against a peril." "I am going thy way. My name is Knowledge." "Scoundrel! Thou art the peril."

A prude is one who blushes modestly at the indelicacy of her thoughts and virtuously flies from the temptation of her desires.

The man who is always taking you by the hand is the same who if you were hungry would take you by the cafe.

When a certain sovereign wanted war he threw out a diplomatic intimation; when ready, a diplomat.

If public opinion were determined by a throw of the dice, it would in the long run be half the time right.

The gambling known as business looks with austere disfavor upon the business known as gambling.

A virtuous widow is the most loyal of mortals; she is faithful to that which is neither pleased nor profited by her fidelity.

Of one who was "foolish" the creators of our language said that he was "fond." That we have not definitely reversed the meanings of the words should be set down to the credit of our courtesy.

Rioting gains its end by the power of numbers. To a believer in the wisdom and goodness of majorities it is not permitted to denounce a successful mob.

Artistically set to grace The wall of a dissecting-place, A human pericardium Was fastened with a bit of gum, While, simply underrunning it, The one word, "Charity," was writ To show the student band that hovered About it what it once had covered.

Virtue is not necessary to a good reputation, but a good reputation is helpful to virtue.

When lost in a forest go always down hill. When lost in a philosophy or doctrine go up-ward.

We submit to the majority because we have to. But we are not compelled to call our attitude of subjection a posture of respect.

Pascal says that an inch added to the length of Cleopatra's nose would have changed the fortunes of the world. But having said this, he has said nothing, for all the forces of nature and all the power of dynasties could not have added an inch to the length of Cleopatra's nose.

Our luxuries are always masquerading as necessaries. Woman is the only necessary having the boldness and address to compel recognition as a luxury.

"I am the seat of the affections," said the heart. "Thank you," said the judgment, "you save my face."

"Who art thou that weepest?" "Man." "Nay, thou art Egotism. I am the Scheme of the

Universe. Study me and learn that nothing matters." "Then how does it happen that I weep?"

A slight is less easily forgiven than an injury, because it implies something of contempt, indifference, an overlooking of our importance; whereas an injury presupposes some degree of consideration. "The blackguards!" said a traveler whom Sicilian brigands had released without ransom; "did they think me a person of no consequence?"

The people's plaudits are unheard in hell.

Generosity to a fallen foe is a virtue that takes no chances.

If there was a world before this we must all have died impenitent.

We are what we laugh at. The stupid person is a poor joke, the clever, a good one.

If every man who resents being called a rogue resented being one this would be a world of wrath.

Force and charm are important elements of character, but it counts for little to be stronger than honey and sweeter than a lion.

Grief and discomfiture are coals that cool: Why keep them glowing with thy sighs, poor fool?

A popular author is one who writes what the people think. Genius invites them to think something else.

Asked to describe the Deity, a donkey would represent him with long ears and a tail. Man's conception is higher and truer: he thinks of him as somewhat resembling a man.

Christians and camels receive their burdens kneeling.

The sky is a concave mirror in which Man sees his own distorted image and seeks to propitiate it.

Honor thy father and thy mother that thy days may be long in the land, but do not hope that the life insurance companies will offer thee special rates.

Persons who are horrified by what they believe to be Darwin's theory of the descent of Man from the Ape may find comfort in the hope of his return.

A strong mind is more easily impressed than a weak; you shall not so readily convince a fool that you are a philosopher as a philosopher that you are a fool.

A cheap and easy cynicism rails at everything. The master of the art accomplishes the formidable task of discrimination.

When publicly censured our first instinct is to make everybody a codefendant.

O lady fine, fear not to lead To Hymen's shrine a clown: Love cannot level up, indeed, But he can level down.

Men are polygamous by nature and monogamous for opportunity. It is a faithful man who is willing to be watched by a half-dozen wives.

The virtues chose Modesty to be their queen. "I did not know that I was a virtue," she said. "Why did you not choose Innocence?" "Because of her ignorance," they replied. "She knows nothing but that she is a virtue."

It is a wise "man's man" who knows what it is that he despises in a "ladies' man."

If the vices of women worshiped their creators men would boast of the adoration they inspire.

The only distinction that democracies reward is a high degree of conformity.

Slang is the speech of him who robs the literary garbage carts on their way to the dumps.

A woman died who had passed her life in affirming the superiority of her sex. "At last," she said, "I shall have rest and honors." "Enter," said Saint Peter; "thou shalt wash the faces of the dear little cherubim."

To woman a general truth has neither value nor interest unless she can make a particular application of it. And we say that women are not practical!

The ignorant know not the depth of their ignorance, but the learned know the shallowness of their learning.

He who relates his success in charming woman's heart may be assured of his failure to charm man's ear.

What poignant memories the shadows bring What songs of triumph in the dawning ring! By night a coward and by day a king.

When among the graves of thy fellows, walk with circumspection; thine own is open at thy feet.

As the physiognomist takes his own face as the highest type and standard, so the critic's theories are imposed by his own limitations.

"Heaven lies about us in our infancy," and our neighbors take up the tale as we mature.

"My laws," she said, "are of myself a part: I read them by examining my heart." "True," he replied; "like those to Moses known, Thine also are engraven upon stone."

Love is a distracted attention: from contemplation Of one's self one turns to consider one's dream.

"Halt!—who goes there?" "Death." "Advance, Death, and give the countersign." "How needless! I care not to enter thy camp tonight. Thou shalt enter mine." "What! I a deserter?" "Nay, a great soldier. Thou shalt overcome all the enemies of mankind." "Who are they?" "Life and the Fear of Death."

The palmist looks at the wrinkles made by closing the hand and says they signify character. The philosopher reads character by what the hand most loves to close upon.

Ah, woe is his, with length of living cursed, Who, nearing second childhood, had no first. Behind, no glimmer, and before no ray— night at either end of his dark day.

A noble enthusiasm in praise of Woman is not incompatible with a spirited zeal in defamation of women.

The money-getter who pleads his love of work has a lame defense, for love of work at money-getting is a lower taste than love of money.

He who thinks that praise of mediocrity atones for disparagement of genius is like one who should plead robbery in excuse of theft.

The most disagreeable form of masculine hypocrisy is that which finds expression in pretended remorse for impossible gallantries.

Any one can say that which is new; any one that which is true. For that which is both new and true we must go duly accredited to the gods and await their pleasure.

The test of truth is Reason, not Faith; for to the court of Reason must be submitted even the claims of Faith.

"Whither goest thou?" said the angel. "I know not." "And whence hast thou come?" "I know not." "But who art thou?" "I know not." "Then thou art Man. See that thou turn not back, but pass on to the place whence thou hast come."

If Expediency and Righteousness are not father and son they are the most harmonious brothers that ever were seen.

Train the head, and the heart will take care of itself; a rascal is one who knows not how to think.

Do you to others as you would That others do to you; But see that you no service good Would have from others that they could Not rightly do.

Taunts are allowable in the case of an obstinate husband: balky horses may best be made to go by having their ears bitten.

Adam probably regarded Eve as the woman of his choice, and exacted a certain gratitude for the distinction of his preference.

A man is the sum of his ancestors; to reform him you must begin with a dead ape and work downward through a million graves. He is like the lower end of a suspended chain; you can sway him slightly to the right or the left, but remove your hand and he falls into line with the other links.

He who thinks with difficulty believes with alacrity. A fool is a natural proselyte, but he must be caught young, for his convictions, unlike those of the wise, harden with age.

These are the prerogatives of genius: To know without having learned; to draw just conclusions from unknown premises; to discern the soul of things.

Although one love a dozen times, yet will the latest love seem the first. He who says he has loved twice has not loved once.

Men who expect universal peace through invention of destructive weapons of war are no wiser than one who, noting the improvement of agricultural implements, should prophesy an end to the tilling of the soil.

To parents only, death brings an inconsolable sorrow. When the young die and the old live, nature's machinery is working with the friction that we name grief.

Empty wine bottles have a bad opinion of women.

Civilization is the child of human ignorance and conceit. If Man knew his insignificance in the scheme of things he would not think it worth while to rise from barbarity to enlightenment. But it is only through enlightenment that he can know.

Along the road of life are many pleasure resorts, but think not that by tarrying in them you will take more days to the journey. The day of your arrival is already recorded.

The most offensive egotist is he that fears to say "I" and "me." "It will probably rain"—that is dogmatic. "I think it will rain"—that is natural and modest. Montaigne is the most delightful of essayists because so great is his humility that he does not think it important that we see not Montaigne. He so forgets himself that he employs no artifice to make us forget him.

On fair foundations Theocrats unwise Rear superstructures that offend the skies. "Behold," they cry, "this pile so fair and tall! Come dwell within it and be happy all." But they alone inhabit it, and find, Poor fools, 'tis but a prison for the mind.

If thou wilt not laugh at a rich man's wit thou art an anarchist, and if thou take not his word thou shalt take nothing that he hath. Make haste, therefore, to be civil to thy betters, and so prosper, for prosperity is the foundation of the state.

Death is not the end; there remains the litigation over the estate.

When God makes a beautiful woman, the devil opens a new register.

When Eve first saw her reflection in a pool, she sought Adam and accused him of infidelity.

"Why dost thou weep?" "For the death of my wife. Alas! I shall never again see her!" "Thy wife will never again see thee, yet she does not weep."

What theology is to religion and jurisprudence to justice, etiquette is to civility.

"Who art thou that despite the piercing cold and thy robe's raggedness seemest to enjoy thyself?" "Naught else is enjoyable—I am Contentment." "Ha! thine must be a magic shirt. Off with it! I shiver in my fine attire." "I have no shirt. Pass on, Success."

Ignorance when inevitable is excusable. It may be harmless, even beneficial; but it is charming only to the unwise. To affect a spurious ignorance is to disclose a genuine.

Because you will not take by theft what you can have by cheating, think not yours is the only conscience in the world. Even he who permits you to cheat his neighbor will shrink from permitting you to cheat himself.

"God keep thee, stranger; what is thy name?" "Wisdom. And thine?" "Knowledge. How does it happen that we meet?" "This is an intersection of our paths." "Will it ever be decreed that we travel always the same road?" "We were well named if we knew."

Nothing is more logical than persecution. Religious tolerance is a kind of infidelity.

Convictions are variable; to be always consistent is to be sometimes dishonest.

The philosopher's profoundest conviction is that which he is most reluctant to express, lest he mislead.

When exchange of identities is possible, be careful; you may choose a person who is willing.

The most intolerant advocate is he who is trying to convince himself.

In the Parliament of Otumwee the Chancellor of the Exchequer proposed a tax on fools. "The right honorable and generous gentleman," said a member, "forgets that we already have it in the poll tax."

"Whose dead body is that?" "Credulity's." "By whom was he slain?" "Credulity." "Ah, suicide." "No, surfeit. He dined at the table of Science, and swallowed all that was set before him."

Don't board with the devil if you wish to be fat.

Pray do not despise your delinquent debtor; his default is no proof of poverty.

Courage is the acceptance of the gambler's chance: a brave man bets against the game of the gods.

"Who art thou?" "A philanthropist. And thou?" "A pauper." "Away! you have nothing to relieve my needs."

Youth looks forward, for nothing is behind! Age backward, for nothing is before.

ABOUT THE AUTHOR

As part of our mission to publish great works of literary fiction and nonfiction, Colour the Classics Publishing Corp. is extremely dedicated to bringing to the forefront the amazing works of long dead and truly talented authors. Connect with us!

instagram.com/colourtheclassics

facebook.com/colourtheclassics